MARY ANNING, FOSSIL HUNTER

by Carter Vance

The Girl on the Beach

Mary's father gently pulled on the rock. It popped out of the cliff wall. He handed it to Mary. She traced the circles in the rock.

It wasn't always a rock. It was once a sea creature. Long ago, it was buried in mud. The mud kept the creature in perfect shape. It became a fossil.

Rocks and sand piled over the fossil. The rocks grew into cliffs. Mary and her father found the fossil on the cliffs.

Mary Anning was born in 1799. She had an older brother named Joseph. The family lived in England. Their home was near the coast.

Tall cliffs overlooked the sandy shore near their home. Mary often went to the beach. She found many fossils.

Mary and her father kept the best ones. They cleaned them. Then they put them in her father's shop window. Sometimes they sold them.

There were fossils shaped like flowers. Others were shaped like fish. They all fascinated Mary.

She Sells Fossils by the Seashore

Mary's father died in 1810. The family had no money. Life became very hard.

One day, Mary walked along the beach. She found a special fossil. It looked like a ram's horn.

Mary met a woman on the way home. She showed her the fossil. The woman liked it. She bought it from Mary. Mary ran home. She showed the money to her mother.

Now they had an idea. Mary collected fossils. Then her family sold them.

One day, in 1811, Joseph found something. It was a long, thin skull. He thought it was a crocodile head. Joseph knew the body must be nearby. He thought Mary should look for it. It wasn't easy. Strong waves may have washed the rest of the body far from the skull.

Finally, after almost a year, Mary found the skeleton. It was surrounded by rock in the cliffs. It was huge. Workers cut away the rock around the skeleton. Then they carried it into town.

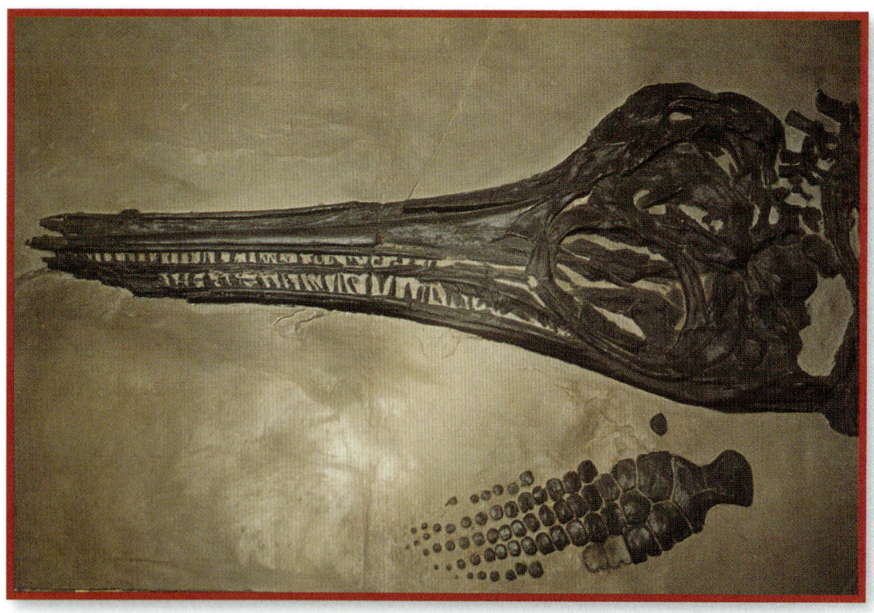

Ichthyosaurus fossil

The skeleton had flippers and very sharp teeth. Scientists named it *ichthyosaurus*. That means "fish lizard." Scientists later realized that it was not a fish. It also was not a lizard. It was a different kind of reptile that swam. It was over two hundred and fifty million years old.

Famous scientists wrote about the fossil. None of them mentioned Mary. Mary was disappointed. Still, the money that Mary got from selling the fossil helped Mary and her family. She could keep looking for fossils.

New Discoveries

Fossil hunters began to visit Mary's beach. She was their guide. She helped them search the sand. She showed them fossils in the cliffs. Everyone agreed that Mary was talented at finding fossils.

People were just learning about the earth. They studied rocks. The rocks told about the earth's age.

People began to apply their ideas to fossils. How old were they? What had these creatures eaten? People studied and did research on Mary's fossils. That led to new ideas.

8

Then Mary shocked the world again. In 1823, she found a new fossil. It was nine feet (2.7m) long and six feet (1.8 m) wide. The head was only five inches (12.7 cm) long!

The creature had four paddles. It was a swimmer. It showed that Mary's ichthyosaurus was not the only ancient sea creature. People called it *plesiosaurus*. That means "almost like a lizard."

Plesiosaurus fossil

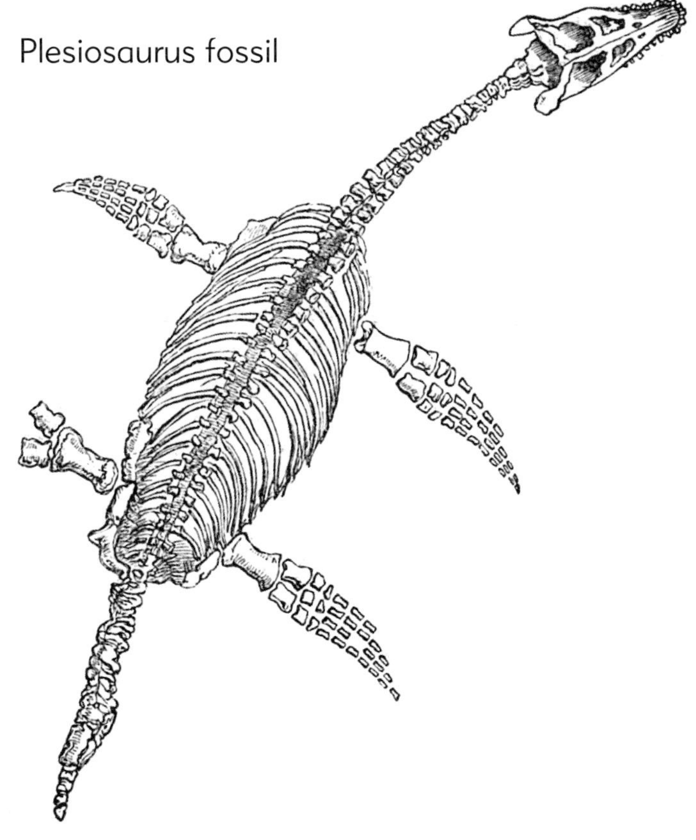

Scientists at that time thought that
creatures from long ago were like the
creatures they knew. The ichthyosaurus
looked like a crocodile. That made sense
to them. The plesiosaurus was different. It
didn't look like anything people knew.

This new fossil raised questions. Maybe
the world had been very different long ago.
Perhaps it could change more. Maybe animals
that lived today could disappear someday.

A Place of Her Own

George Cuvier was a famous fossil expert. He had heard about Mary's latest find. The fossil was strange. He thought she had made it up.

Mary didn't go to a university. She was a woman. People didn't think women could be scientists. It was easy to ignore her.

Then Cuvier saw the drawings of the fossil. He read about how Mary had found it. He read how she had taken it out of the sand. He decided to believe she had found it.

George Cuvier

Cuvier was an important man. He believed in Mary's work. That meant others would, too.

Mary sold the fossil. She now had some money. She bought a house. She opened a fossil shop. Mary had to keep finding fossils to survive. She searched almost every day.

Fossil hunting today is different from long ago

Fossil hunting was not easy. The invention of the jackhammer would come later. Mary only had a chisel. She worked with her bare hands. It took a long time to get to a fossil.

Clothes were also different. Women in those days wore long heavy skirts. She did not let that hinder her, though. She still climbed the rocky cliffs.

Mary died in 1847. The girl on the beach had amazed the science world. She had changed ideas about science and history. To this day, the cliffs where Mary searched are a wonderful place for fossil hunters to explore.

14   Lyme Regis: The town where
      Mary Anning lived

Think Critically

1. What does the part called "A Place of Her Own" tell about?

2. What did ichthyosaurus look like?

3. How do you think Mary felt when no one gave her any credit for her fossil finds?

4. Do you think more people would have paid attention to the fossils if Joseph had found them? Explain your answer.

5. Do you think fossil hunting sounds like fun? Why or why not?

 **Science**

Fossil Facts Look up more information about Mary Anning and the fossils that she found. Make a list of your facts. Share them with the class.

School-Home Connection Tell a family member about the fossils in this book. Discuss other kinds of fossils you may know about.

Word Count: 868 (890)